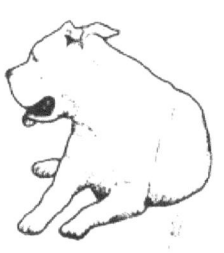

THE SAVANNAH ALPHABET
COLORING BOOK™
BY DAVID LAUGHLIN

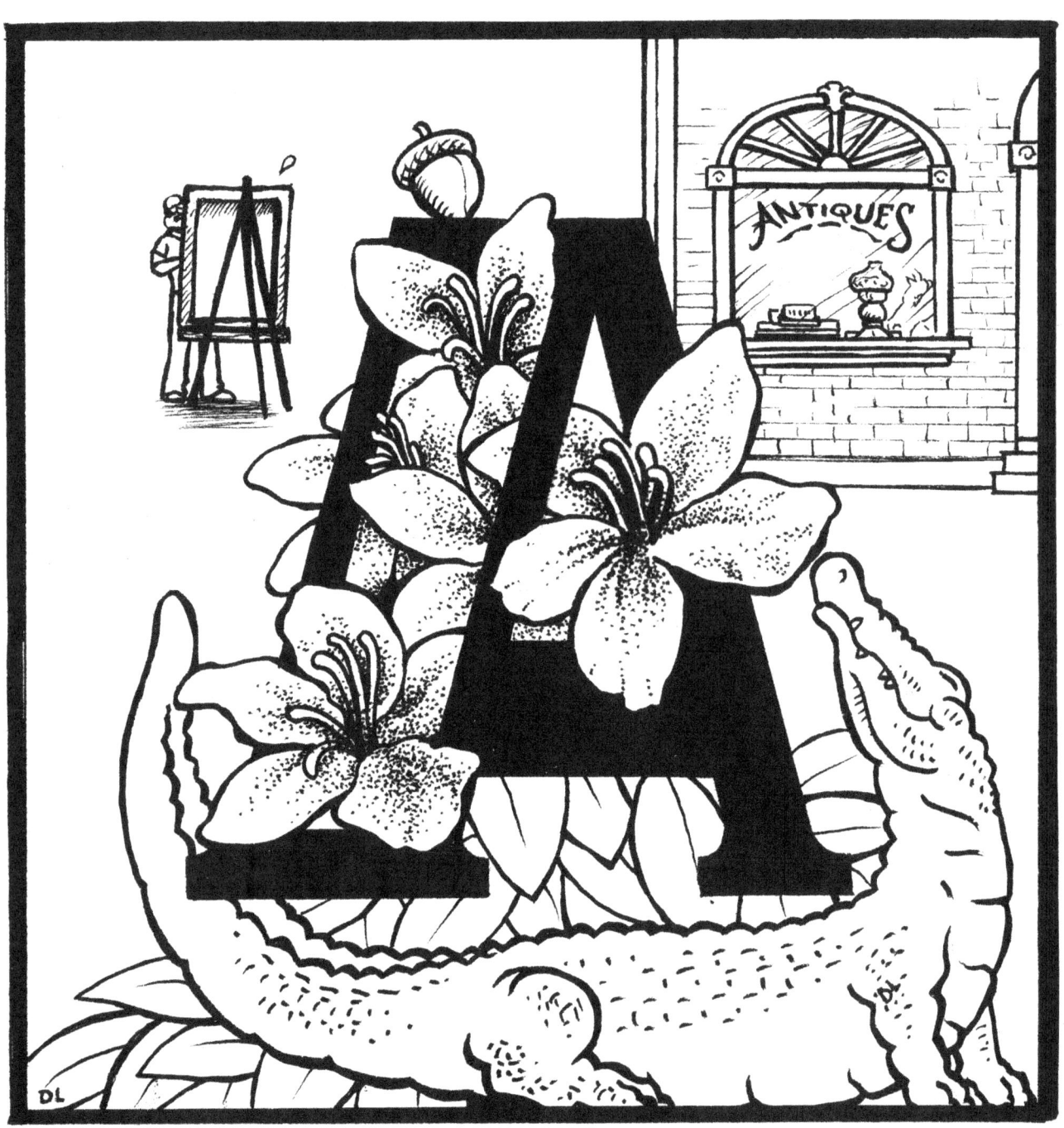

It's a great day for exploring,
or just strolling around.
In Savannah it's always
a nice treat downtown.

There's an old antique shop
near one of the squares nearby
where an artist is working.
Let's see what we can spy.

A is for
Azaleas, antiques, acorn, artist and alligator.

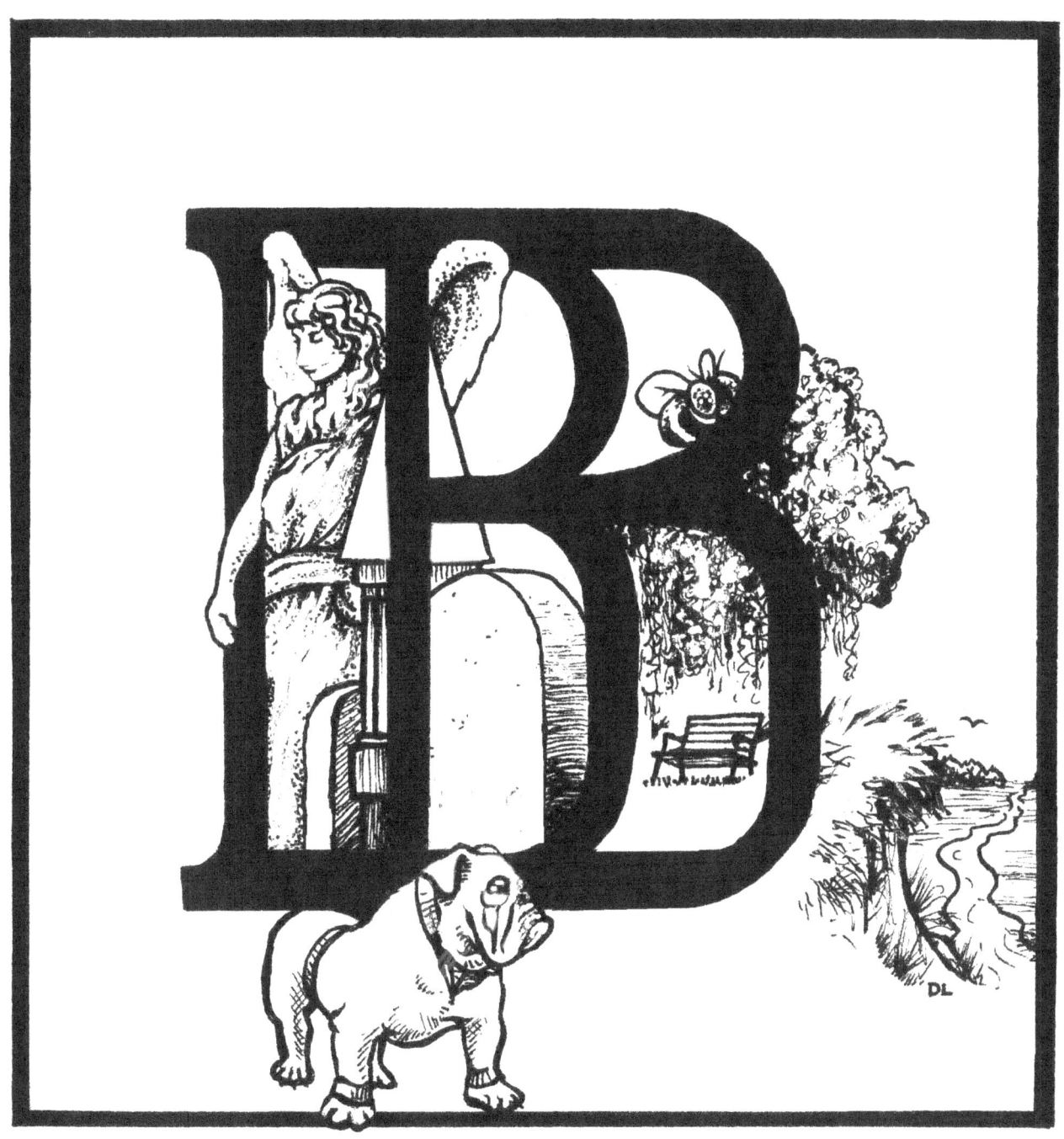

B is for
Bulldog, bench, bluff and bee.
Plus the beautiful
Bonaventure Cemetery.

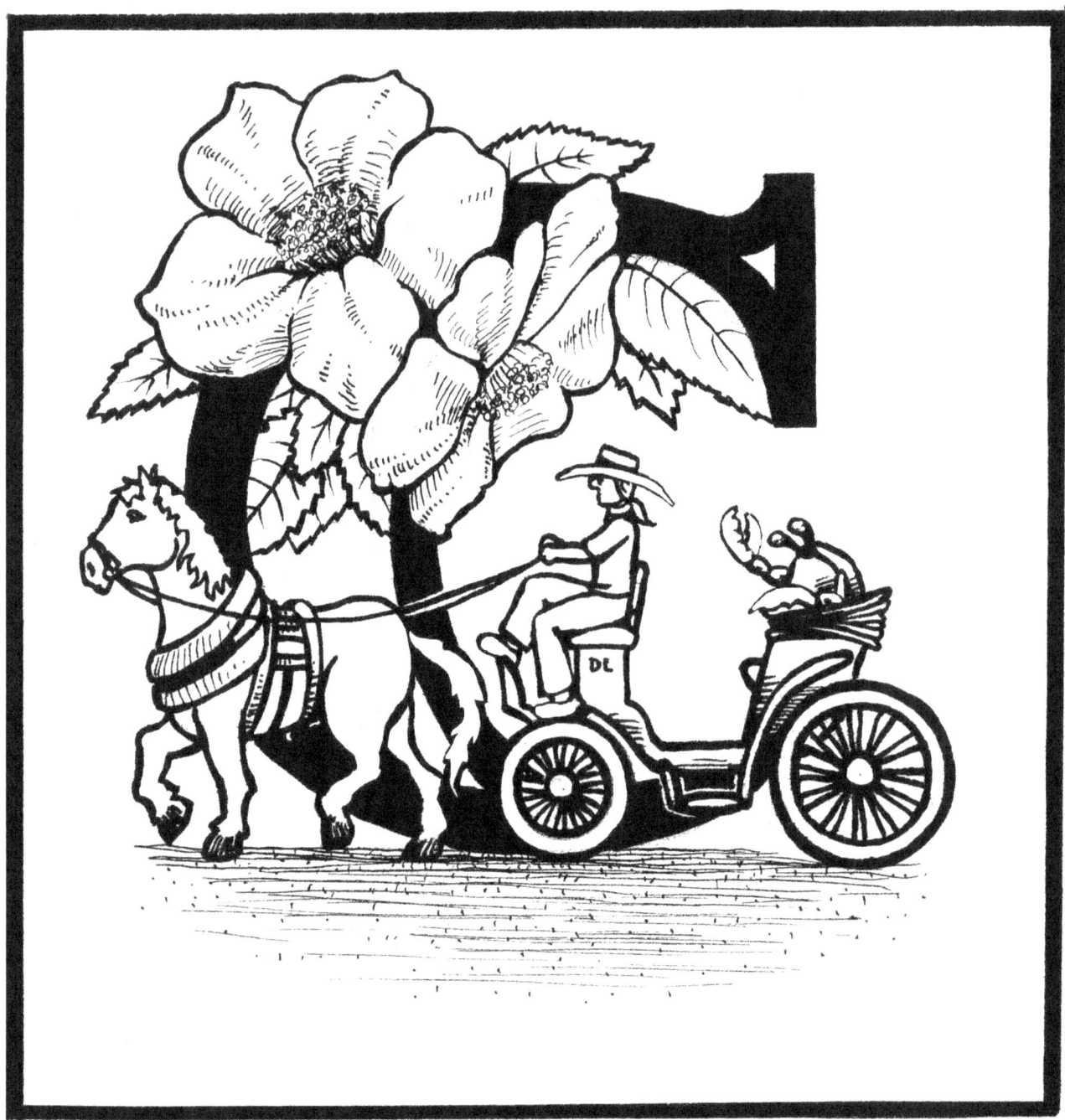

C is for
**Carriage, cobblestones and
the Cherokee Rose.**
The crab's just along for the ride, I suppose.

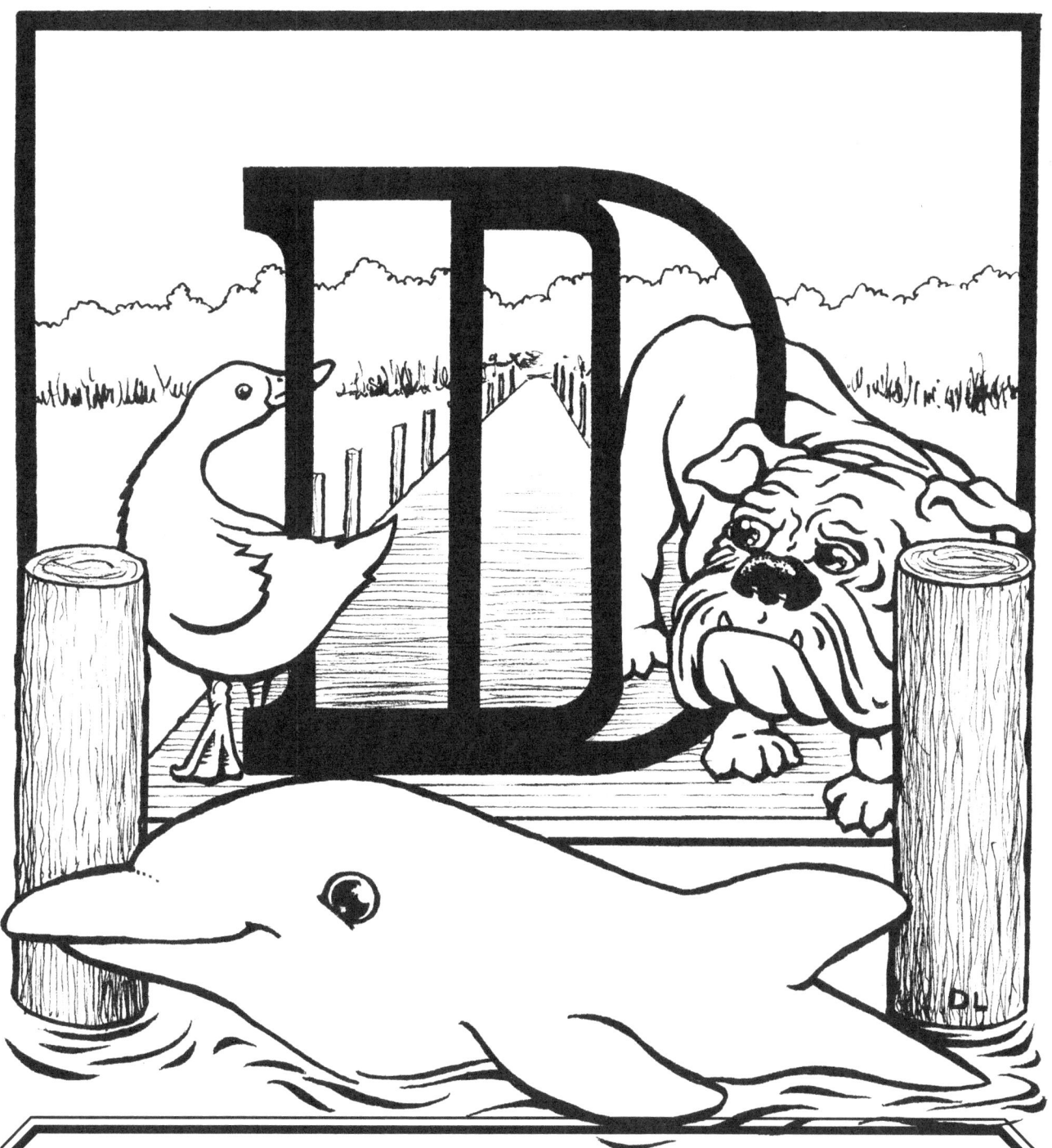

D is for
Dolphin and dock and GO DAWGS too!
The duck is determined
to see who's chasing who.

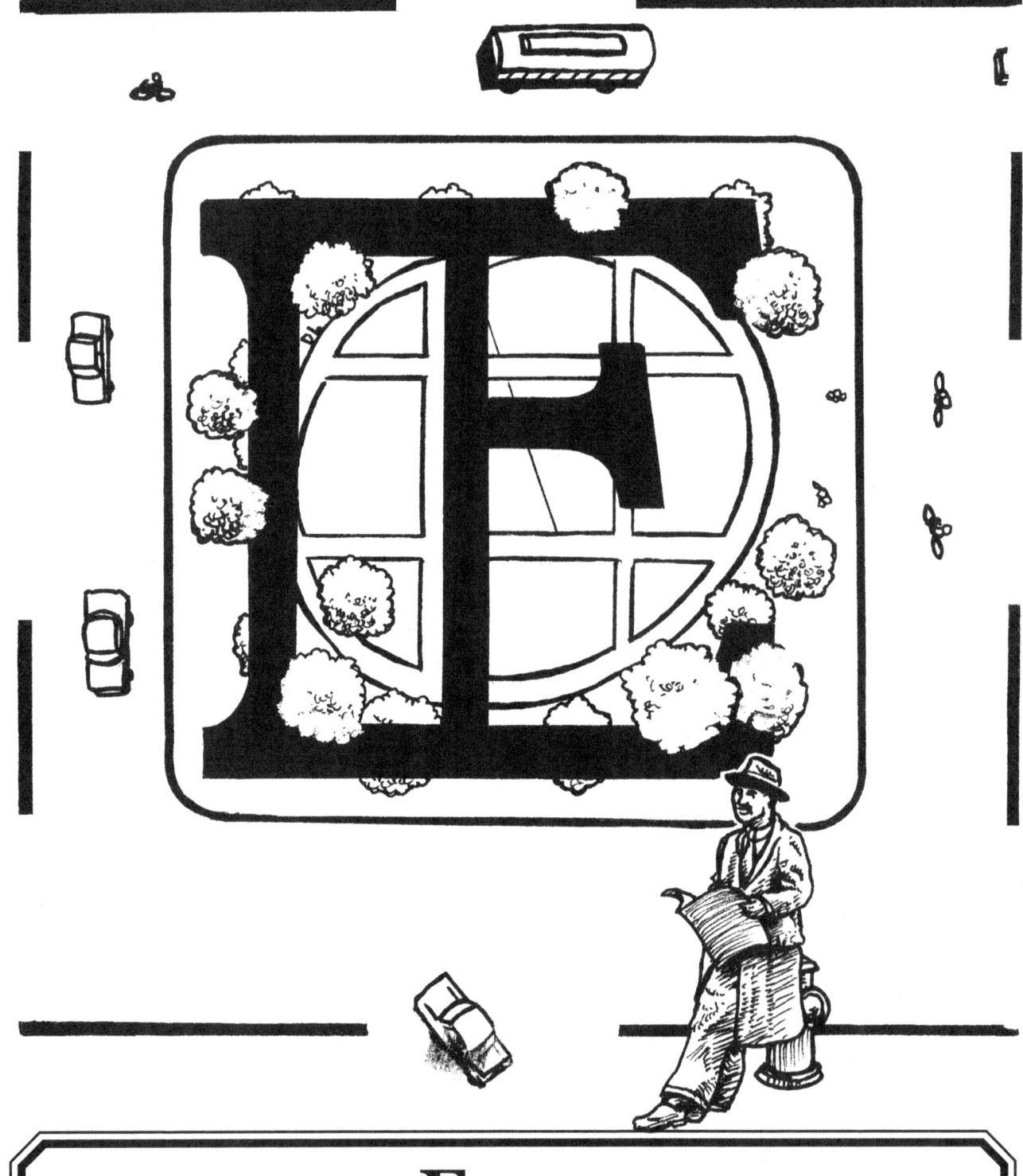

E is for
Ellis Square, there's 24 squares downtown.
Each one is unique and easy to get around.

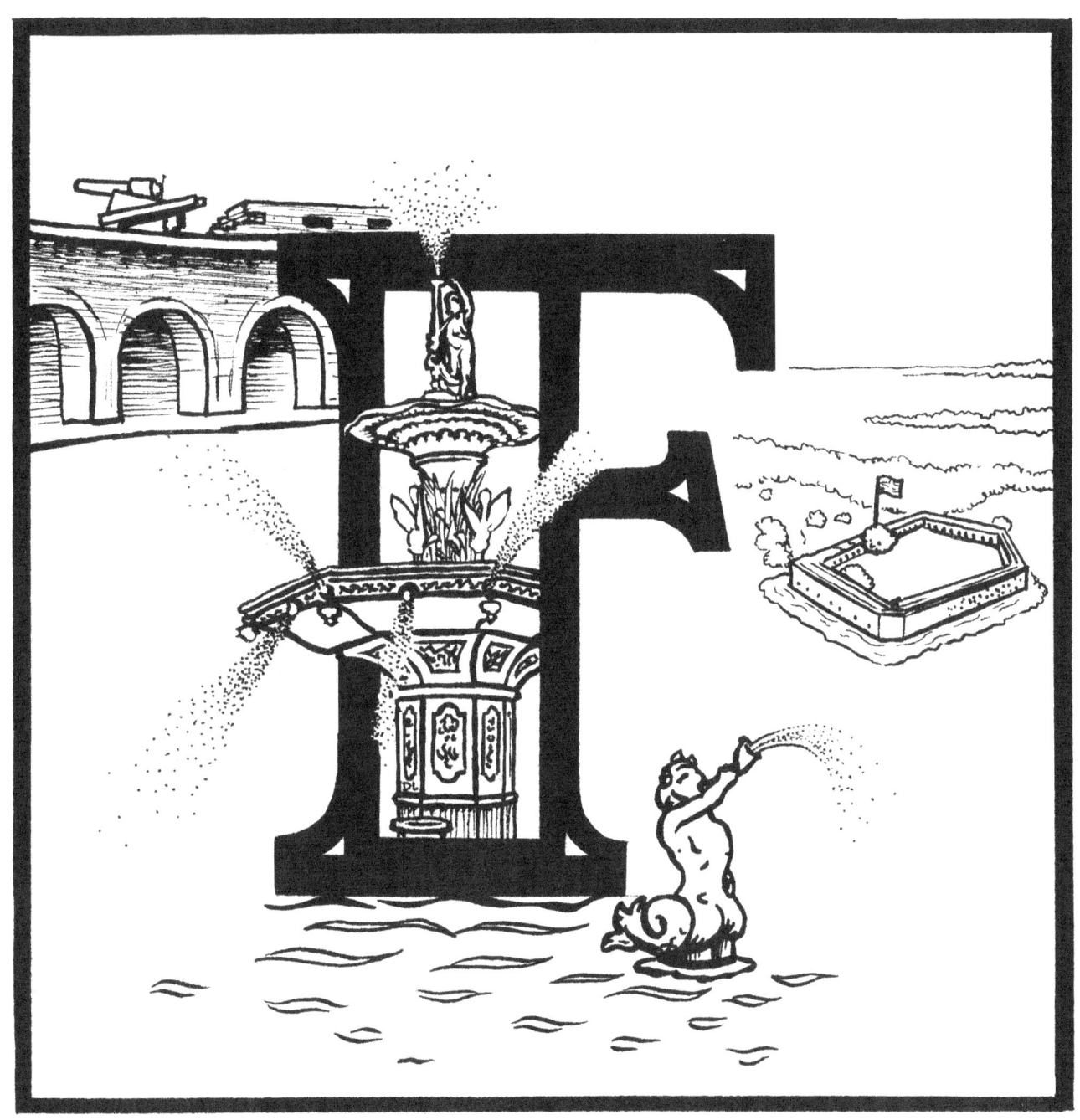

F is for
Fountains, and Forsyth Park too.
The forts are nearby,
so wear good hiking shoes.

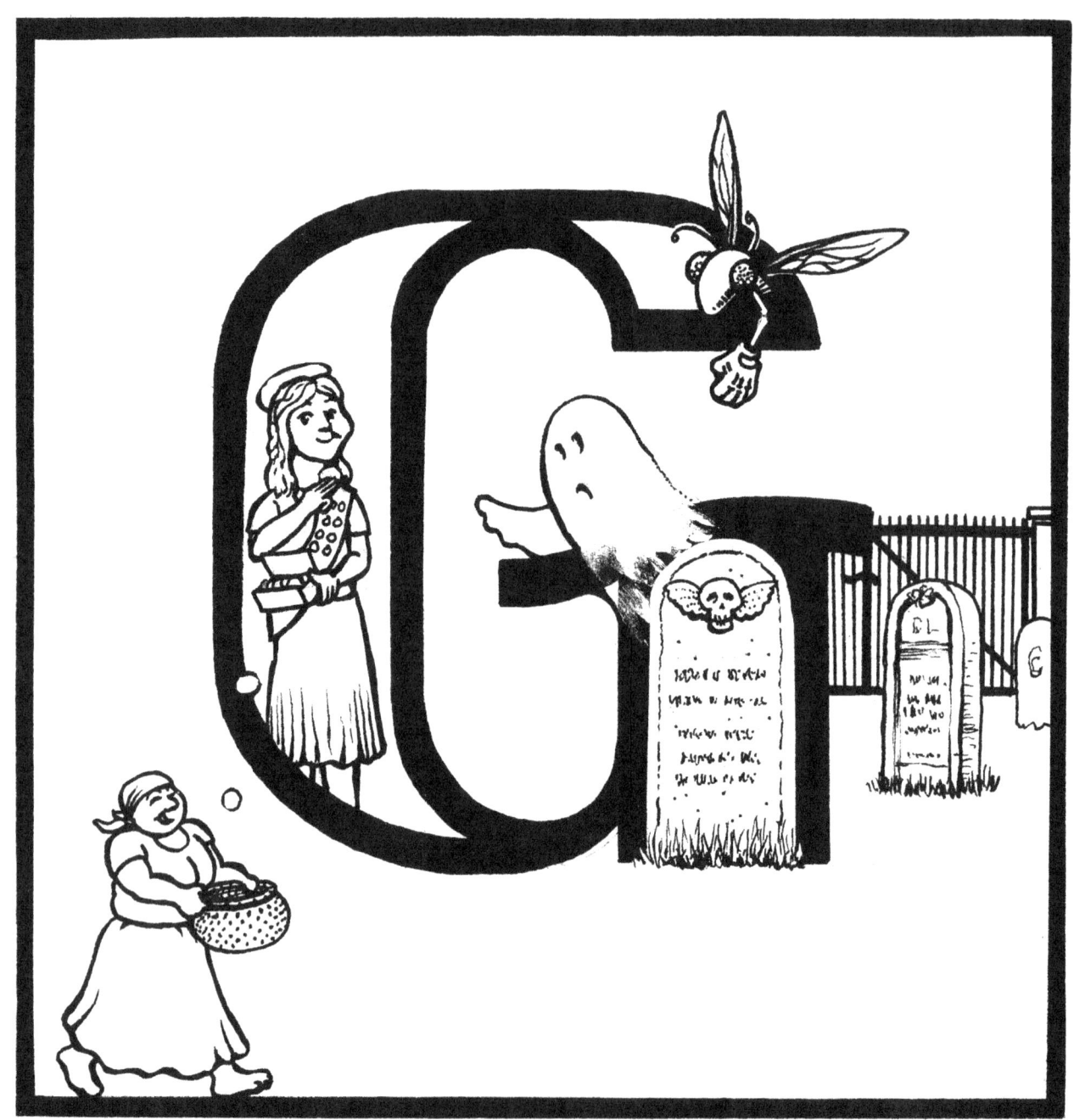

G is for
Gullah, and Gnat, and Girl Scout.
Gravestones and ghosts and
a gate keeps you out.

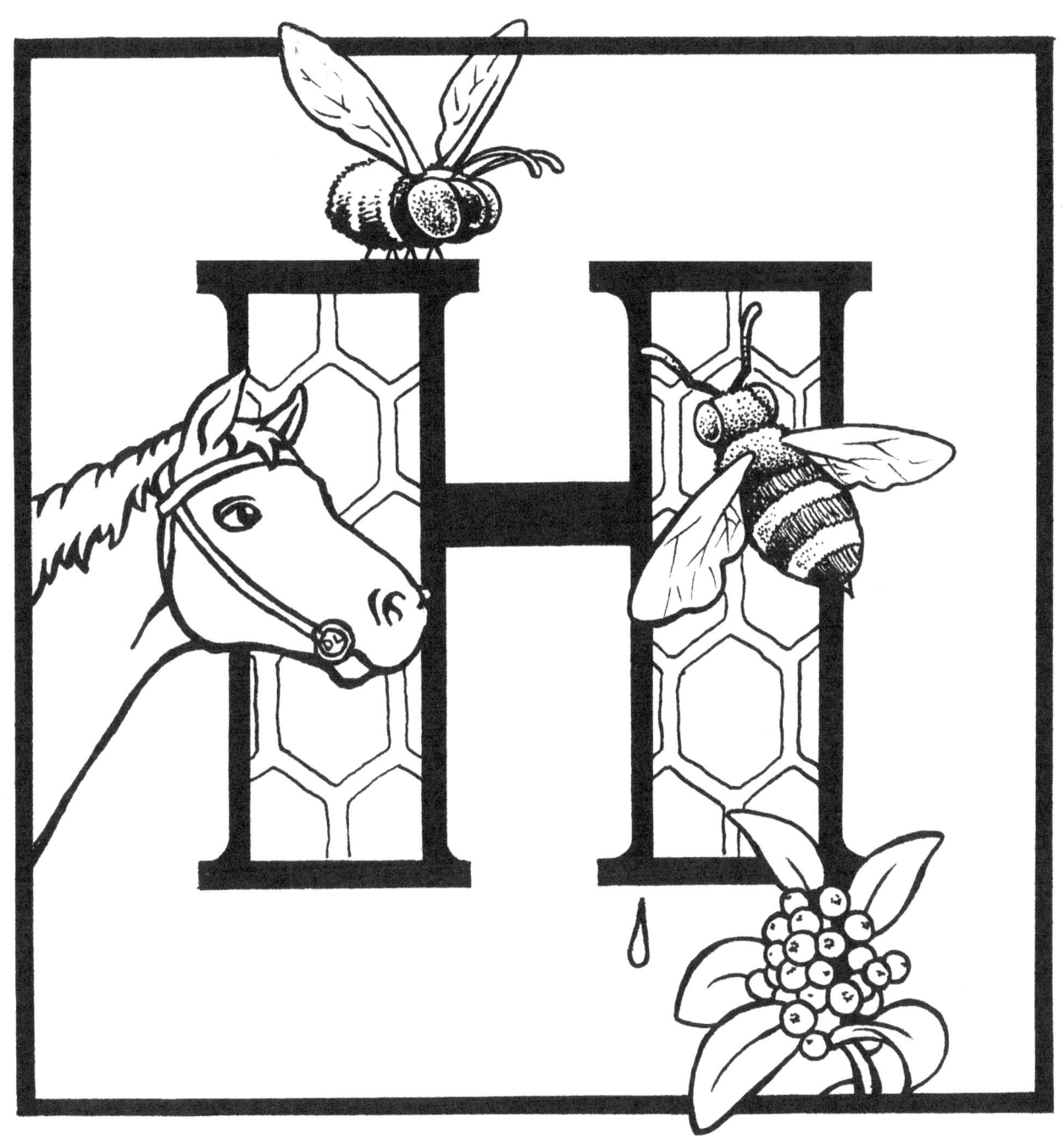

H is for
Honey and honeybees, of courses,
My huckleberry friend,
and don't forget the horses!

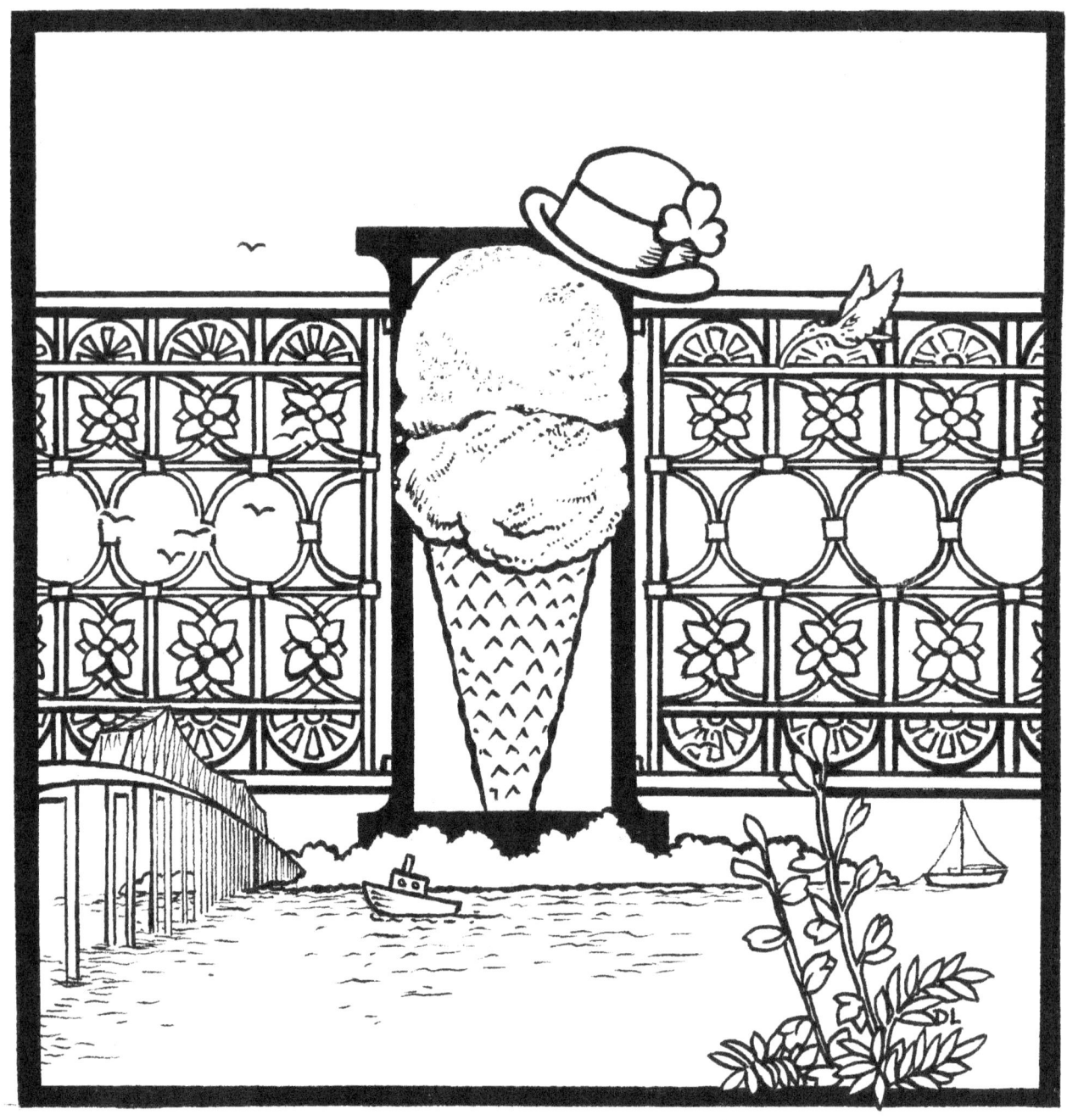

I is for
Irish, ice cream and iron
and indigo grown across the river
on an island.

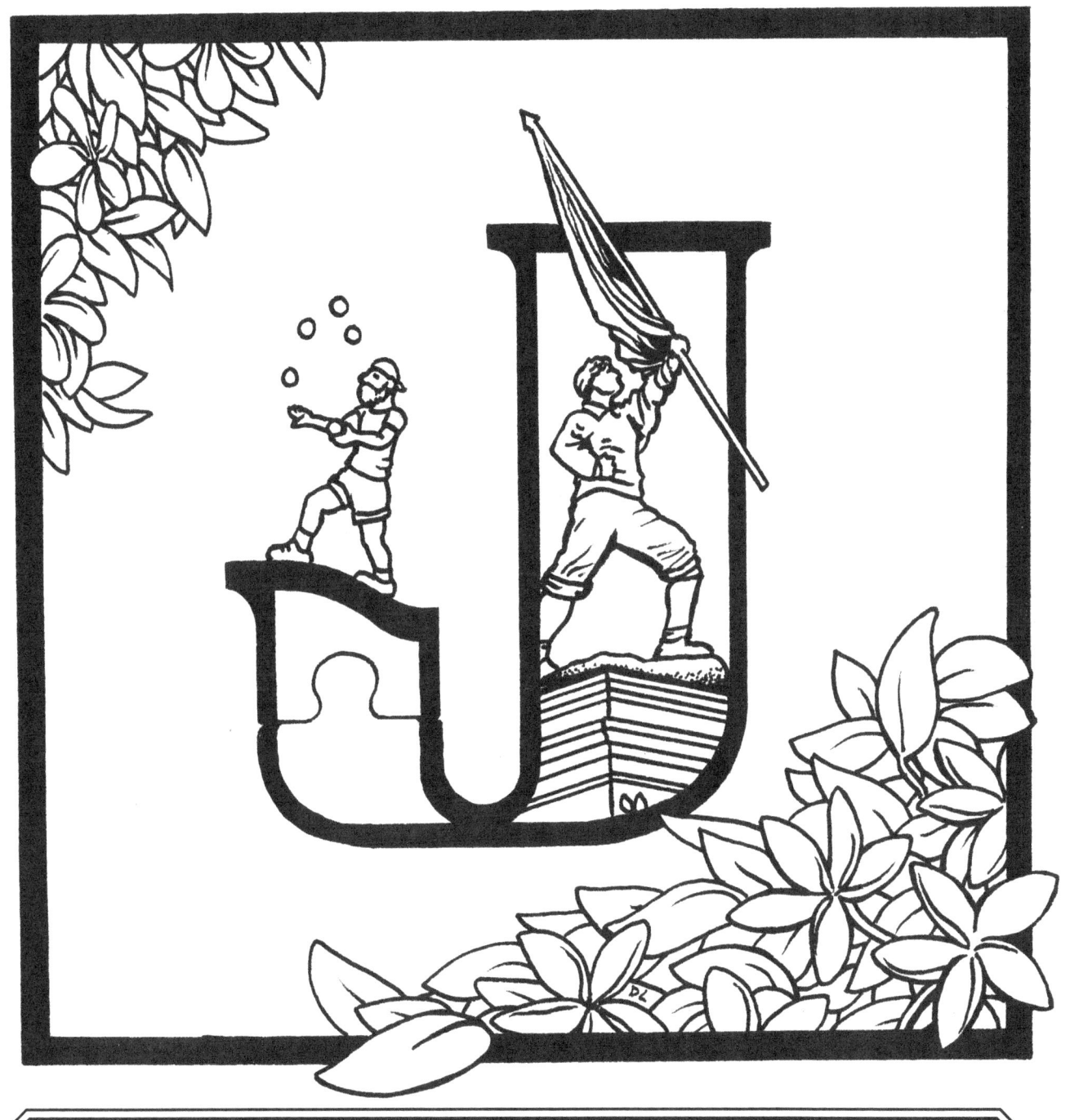

J is for
Jasmine and valiant Sgt. Jasper
On River Street you may see
a juggling performer.

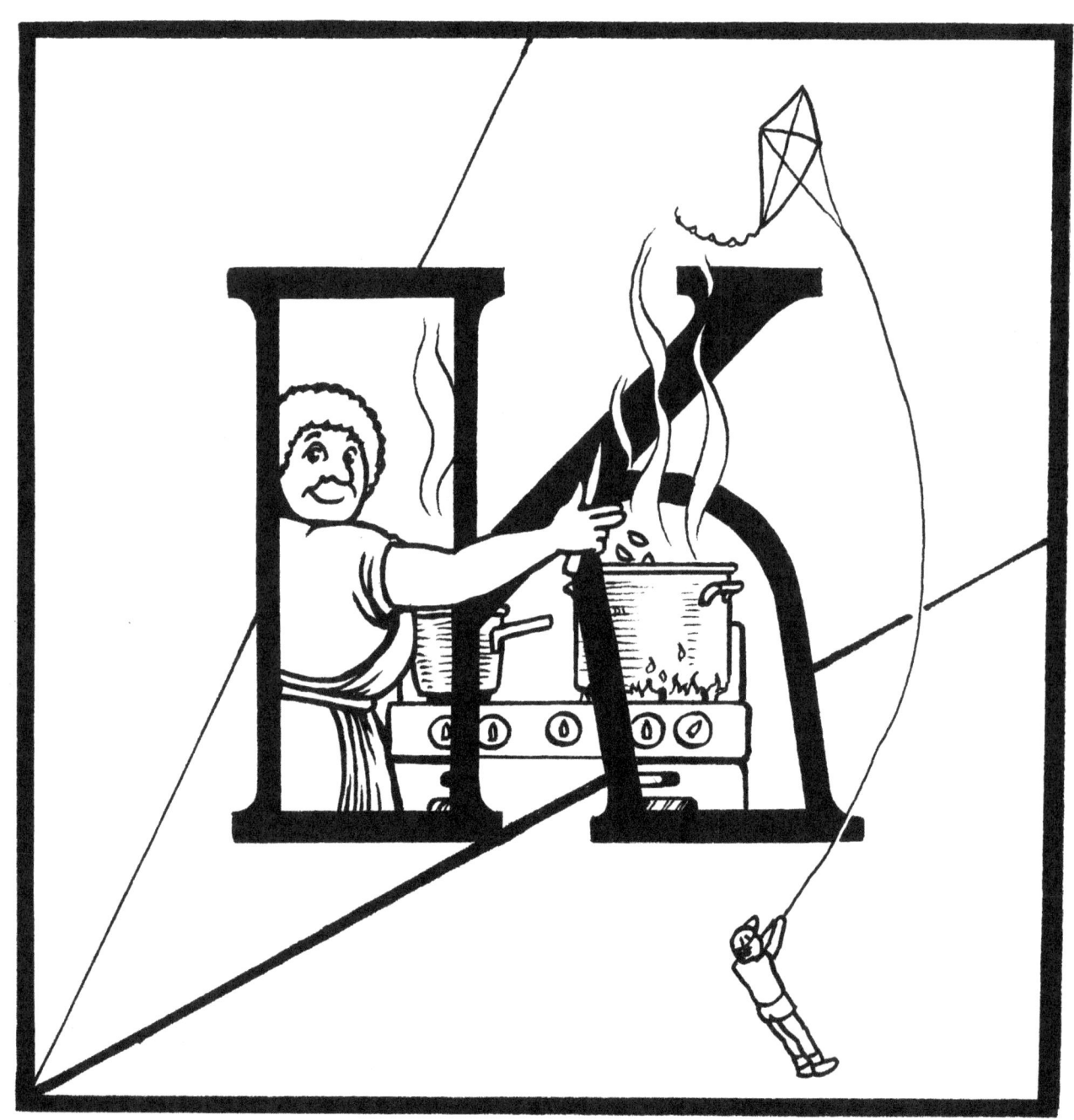

K is for
Kitchen, smells like Brunswick stew.
While you're out flying a kite
someone's cooking for you.

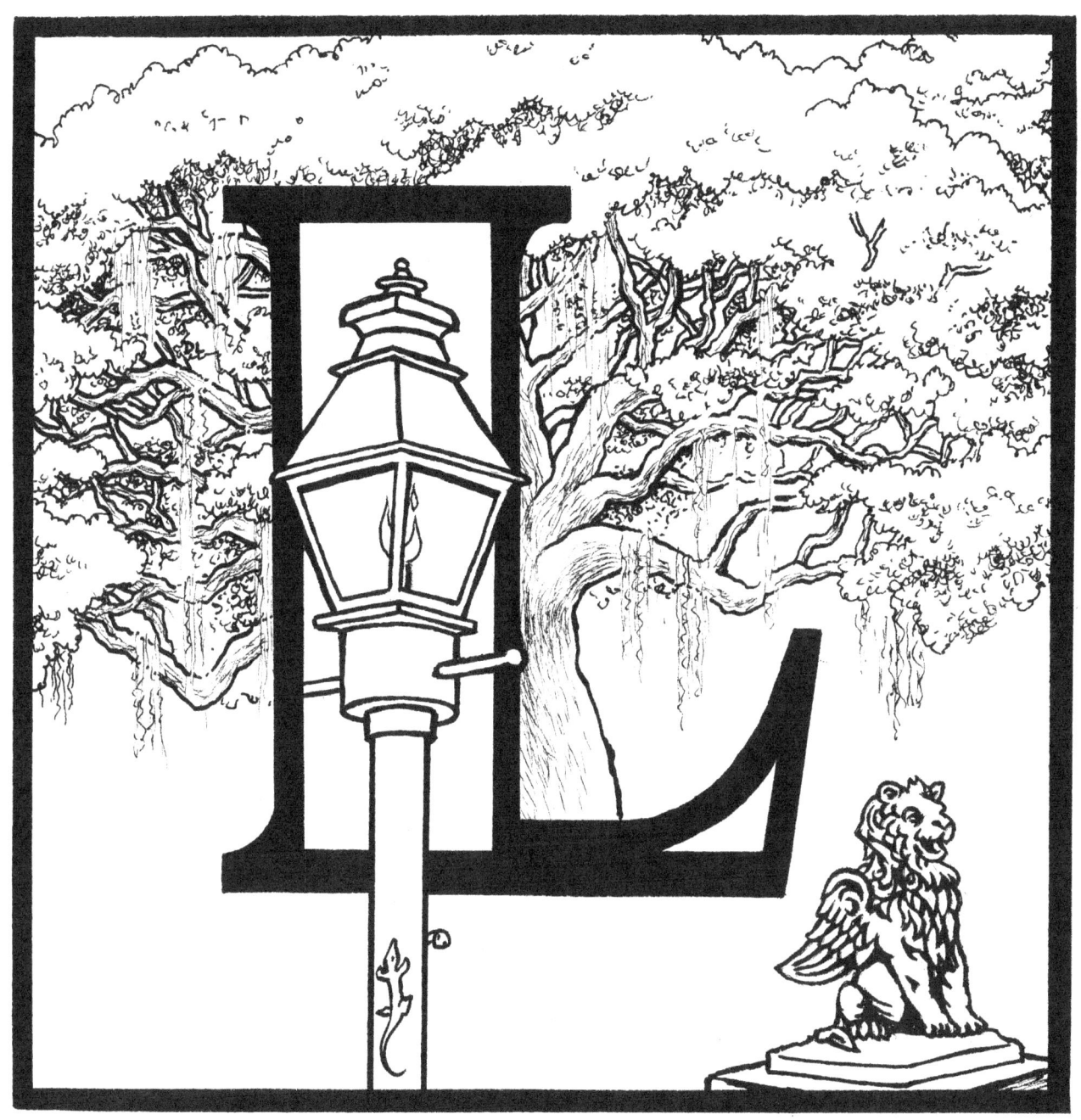

L is for
Live Oaks, which are broad and strong.
The lion is on watch
under gas lamps all night long.

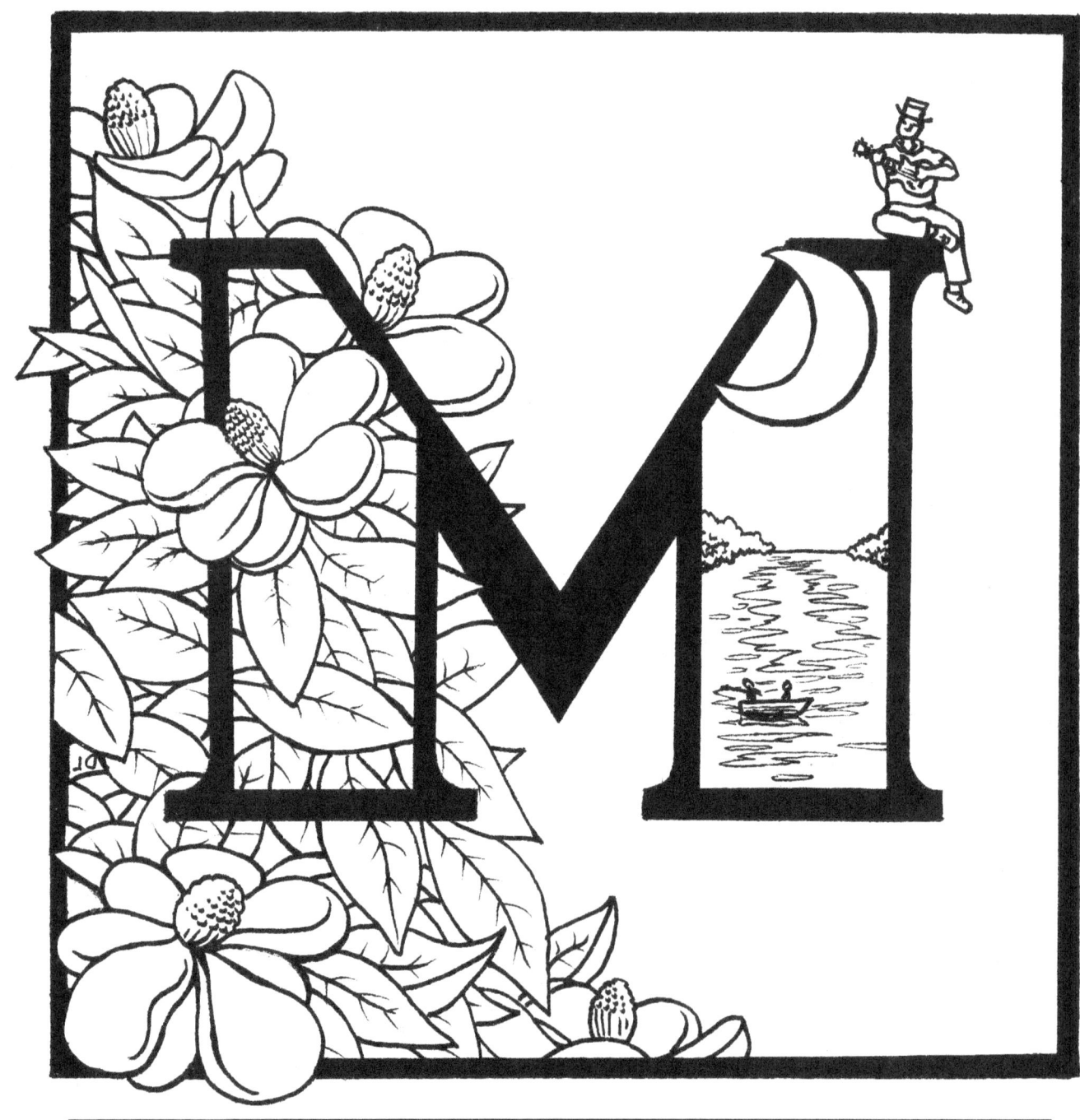

M is for
Magnolia and music and moon.
If I play a mandolin at Moon River
I'll try to stay in tune.

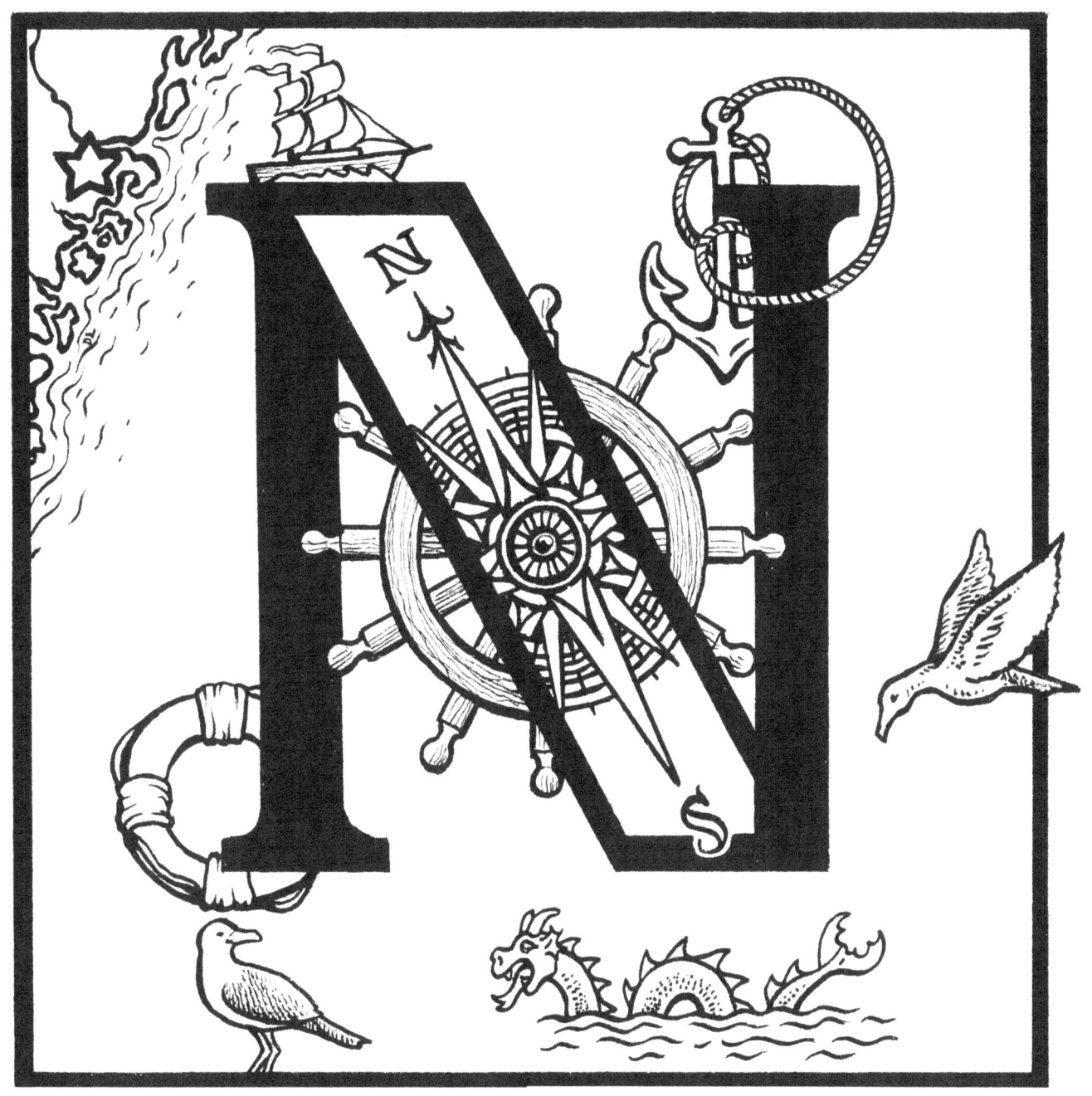

N is for
Nautical, our harbors and waterways.
Whether motor, sail or paddle
We hope you have sunny days.

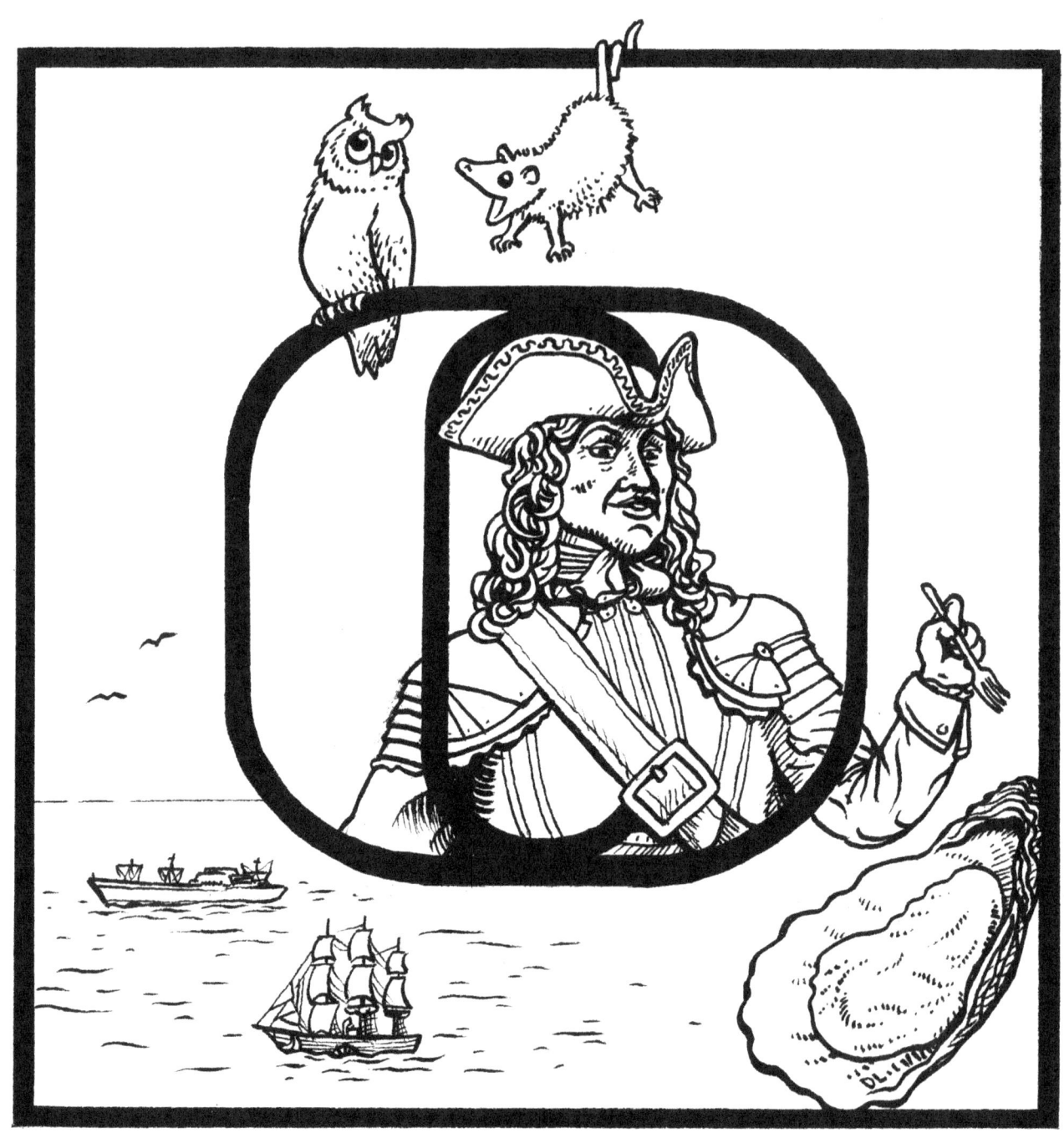

O is for
Oyster and ocean, you see.
Oh, and Gen. Oglethorpe
(the founder of the colony).

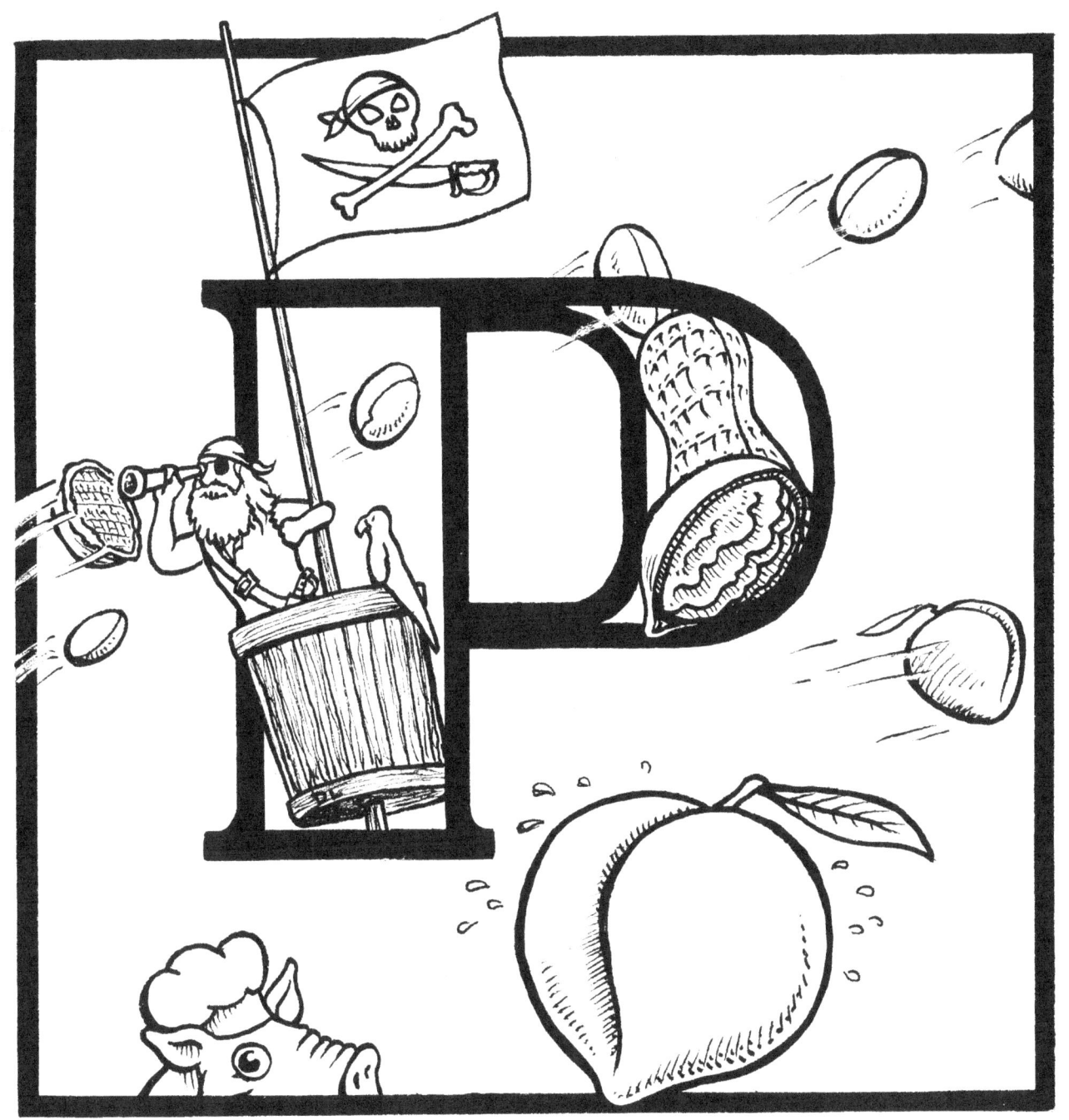

P is for
Peaches, pork, peanuts and pecans.
There's a pie fight at the port
(which actually looks fun).

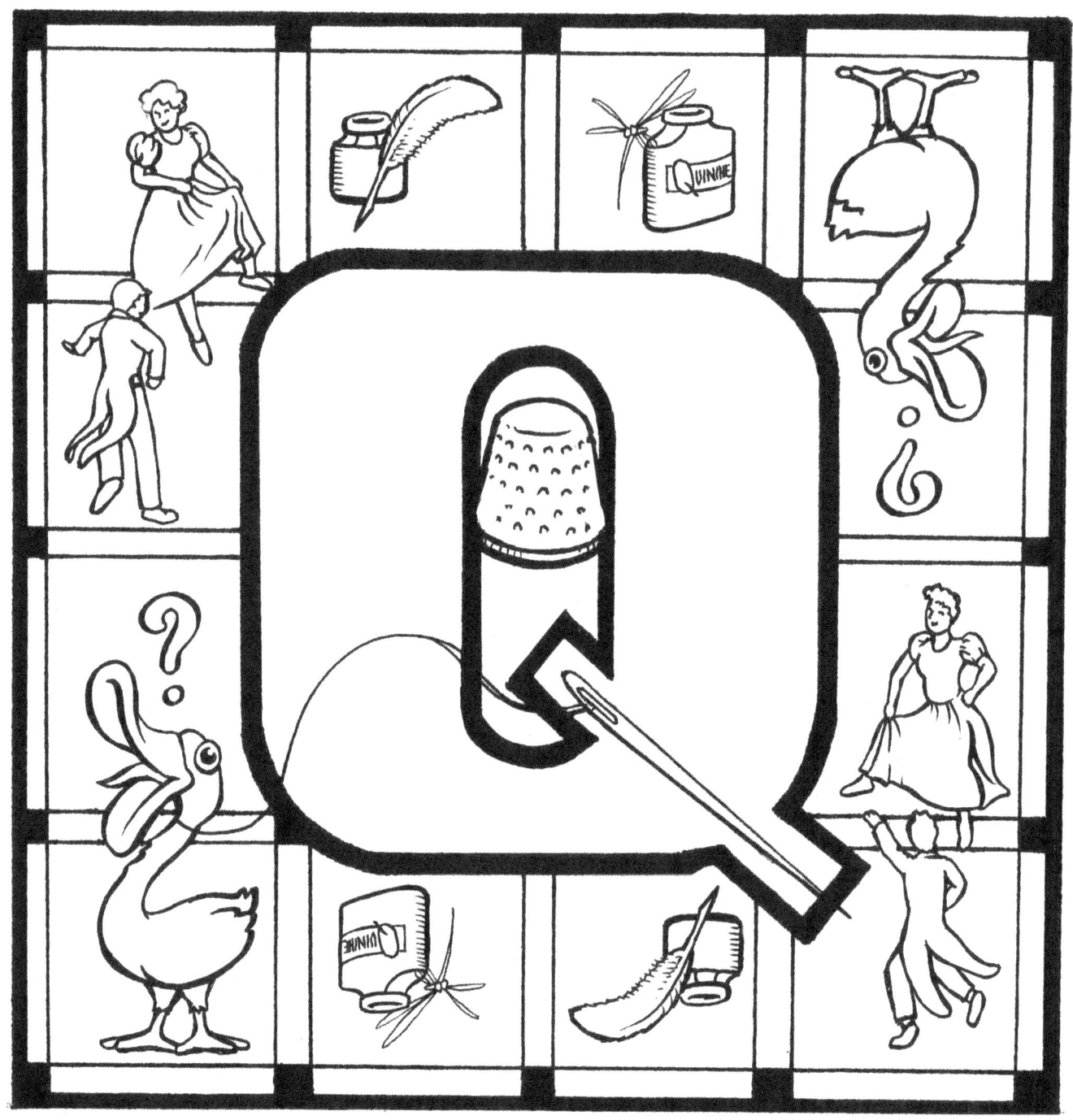

Q is for
**Quilt, quill, quack and quinine.
The quadrille was a dance here
in colonial times.**

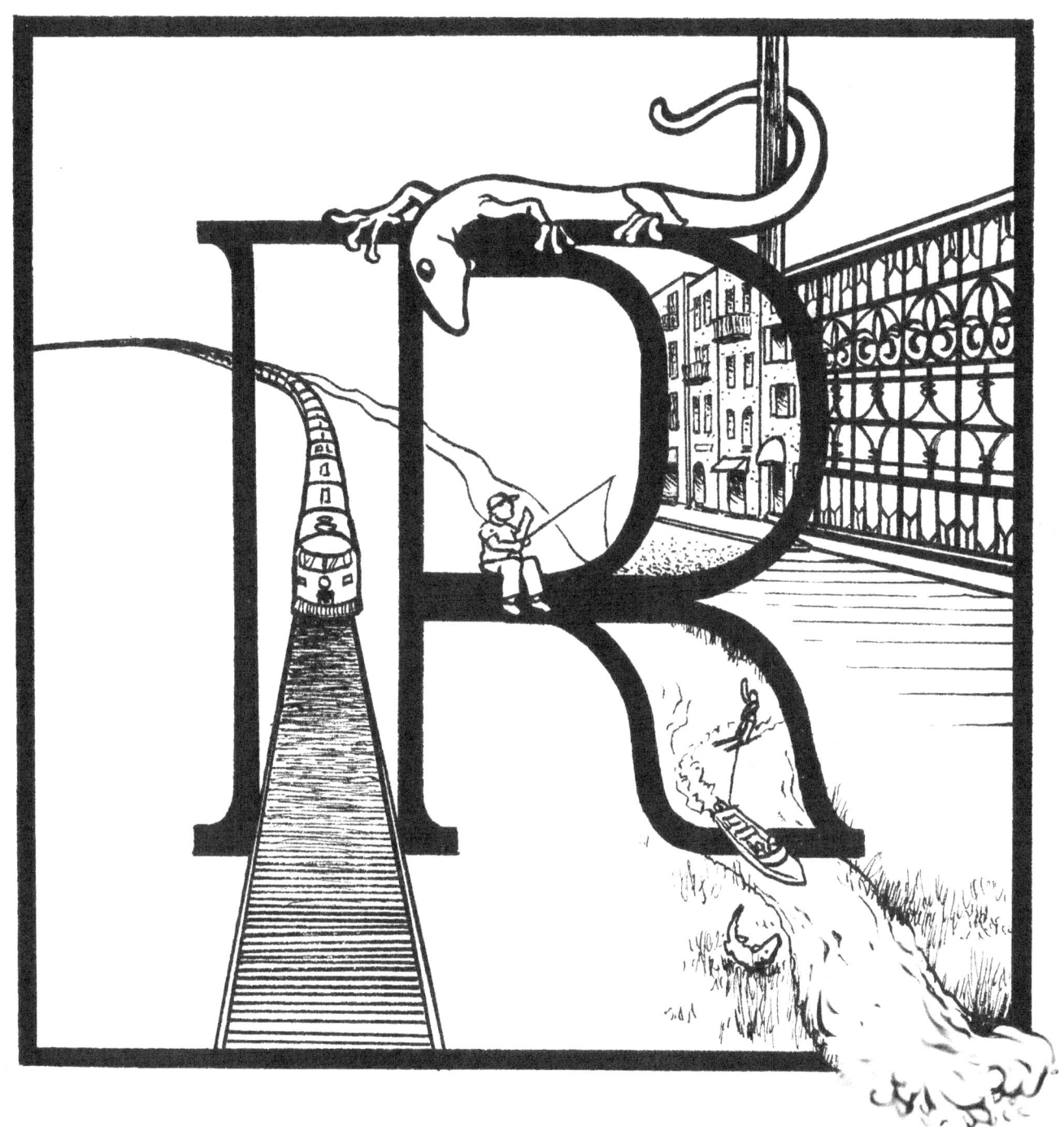

R is for
River, railroad, reptile and rail.
Recreation can be found
somewhere here without fail.

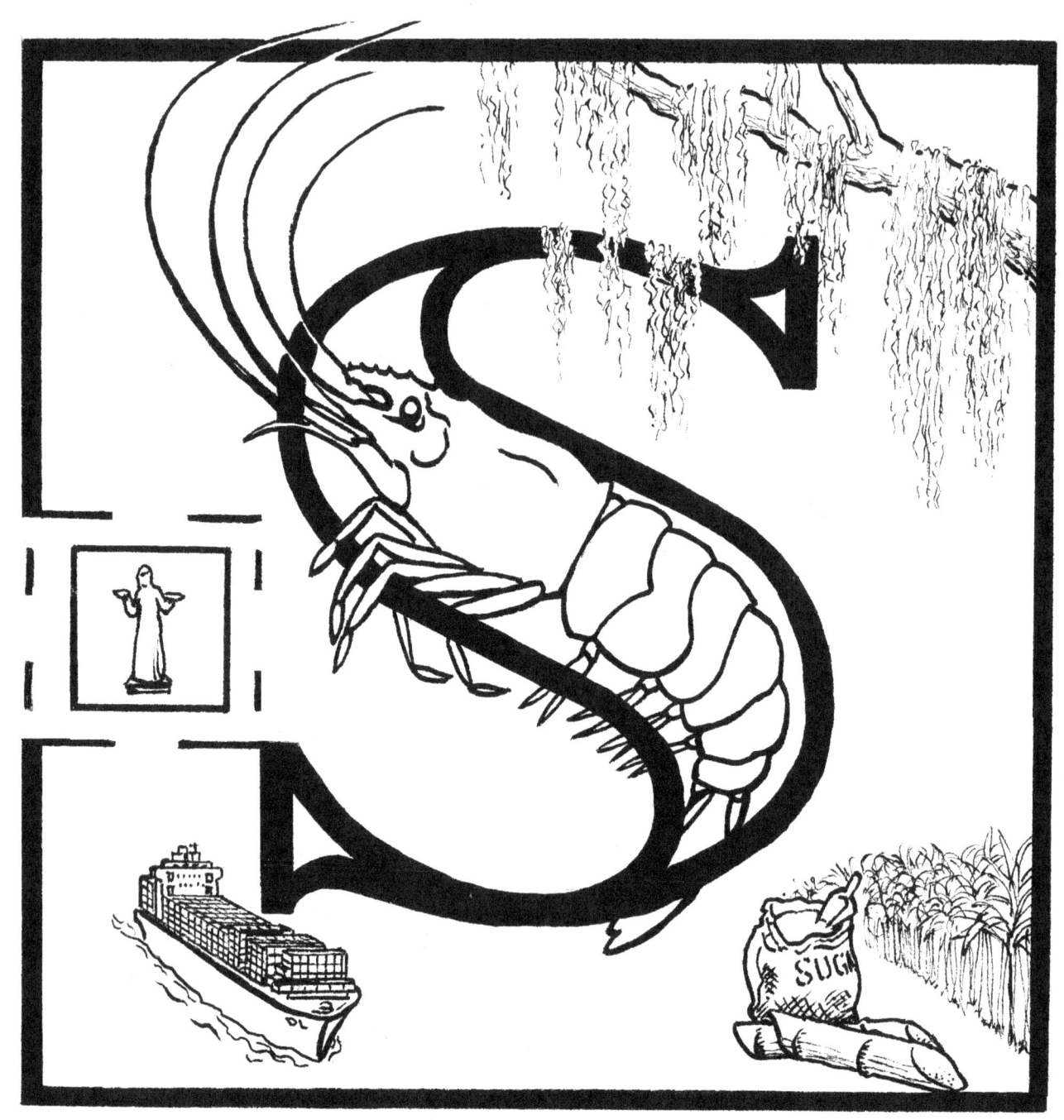

S is for
Shrimp, shipping and sugar cane.
The spanish moss in the squares
over statues and lanes.

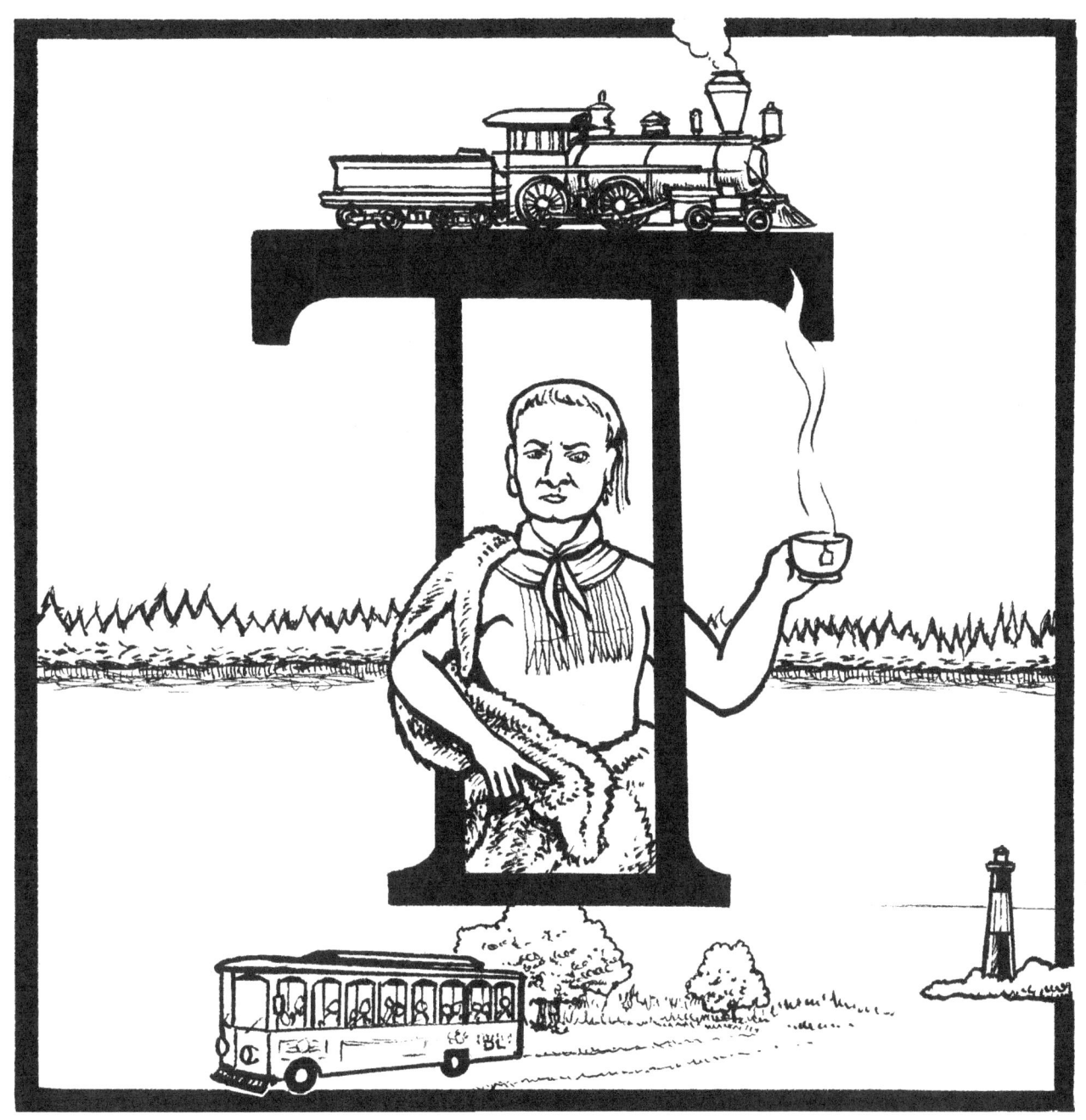

T is for
Tomochichi, trains, trolleys, oh my!
There are trails near the timber
and Tybee Island nearby.

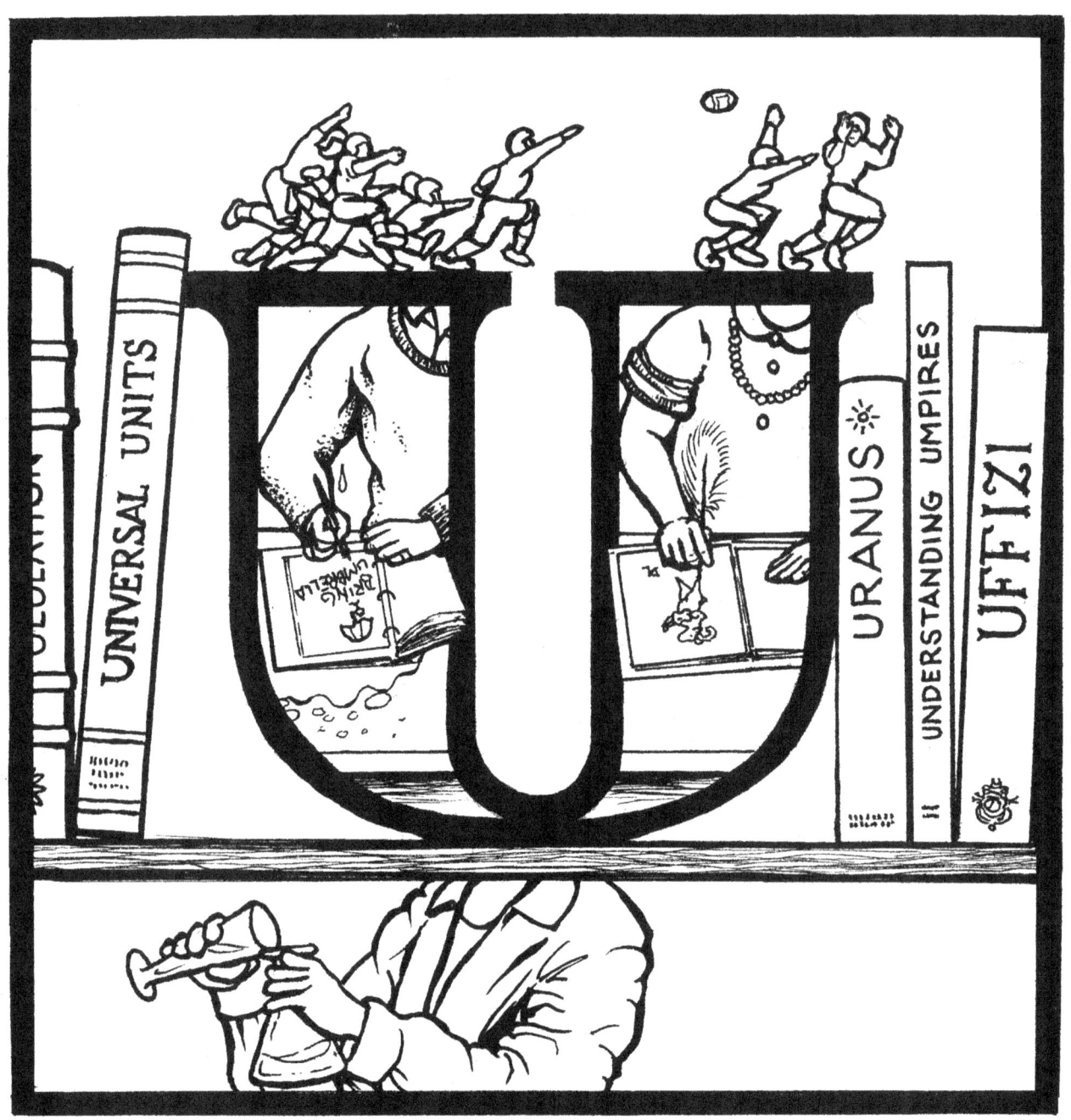

U is for
University, institutions of higher learning.
There are many fields of study here
for your academic journeying.

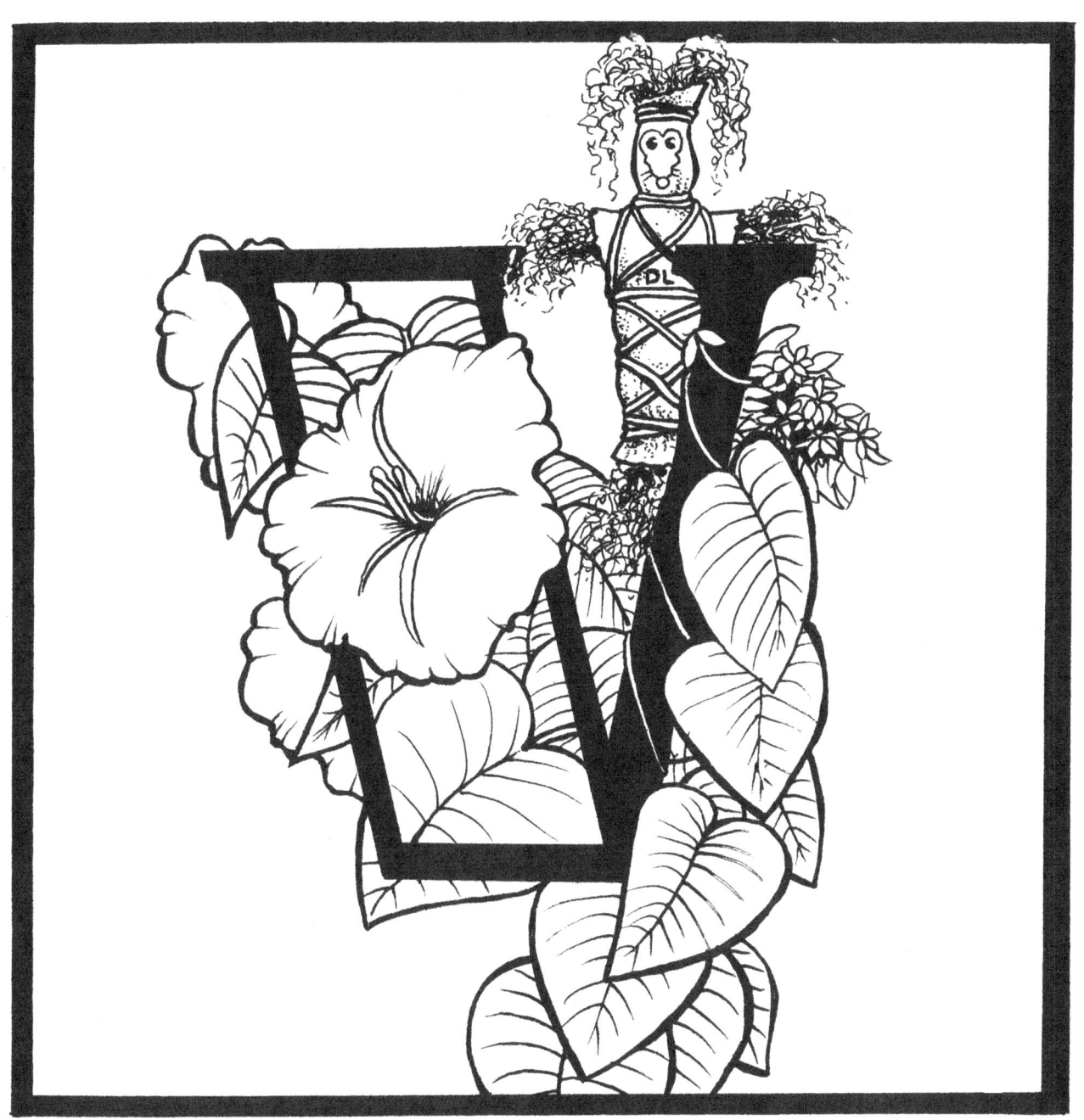

V is for
**Voodoo, vespertine and vine.
When the moonflowers bloom
at night it smells fine.**

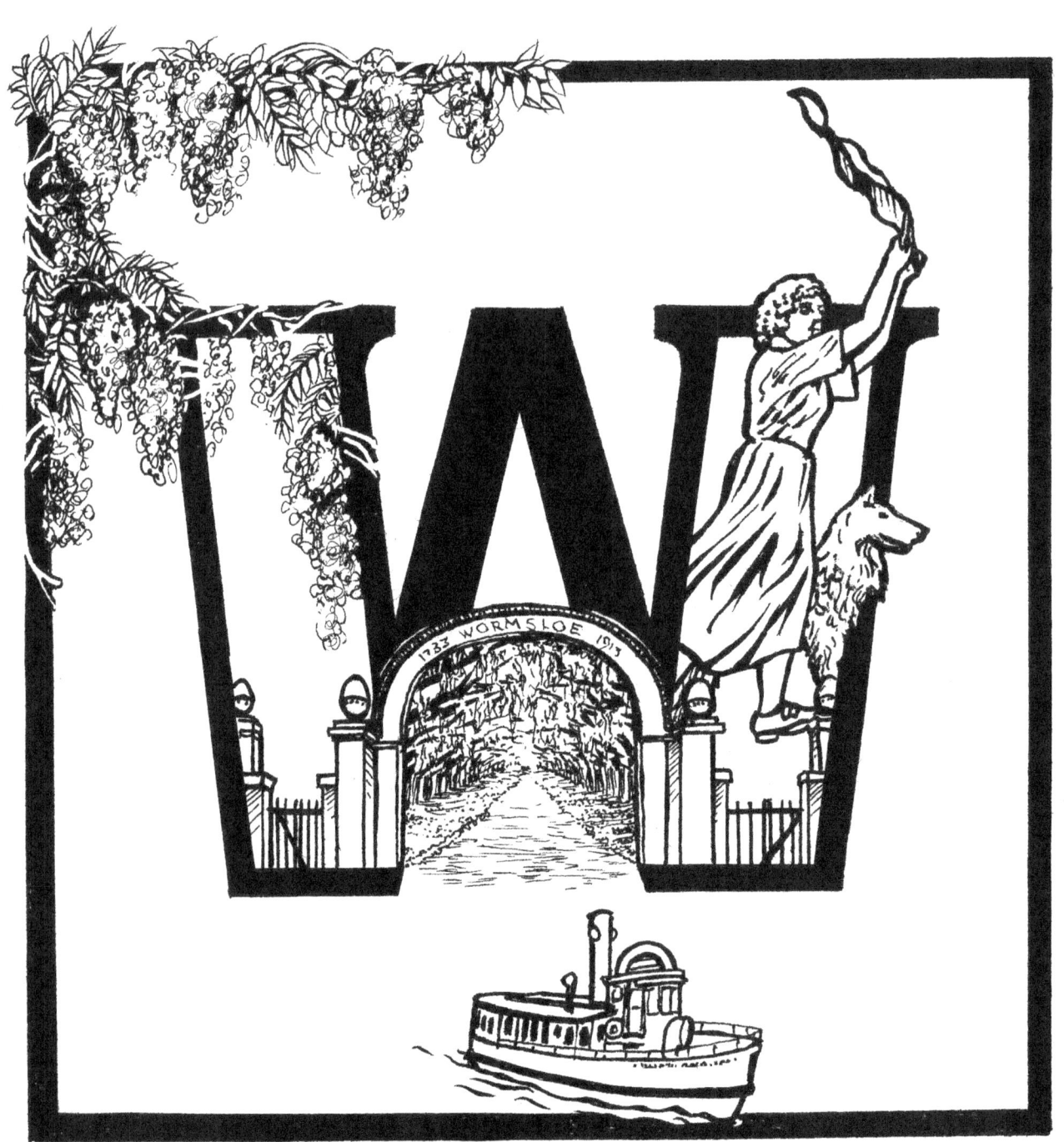

W is for
Wormsloe, it's wide path wandering with oaks.
Water taxi, the waving girl, and
the beauty which wisteria evokes!

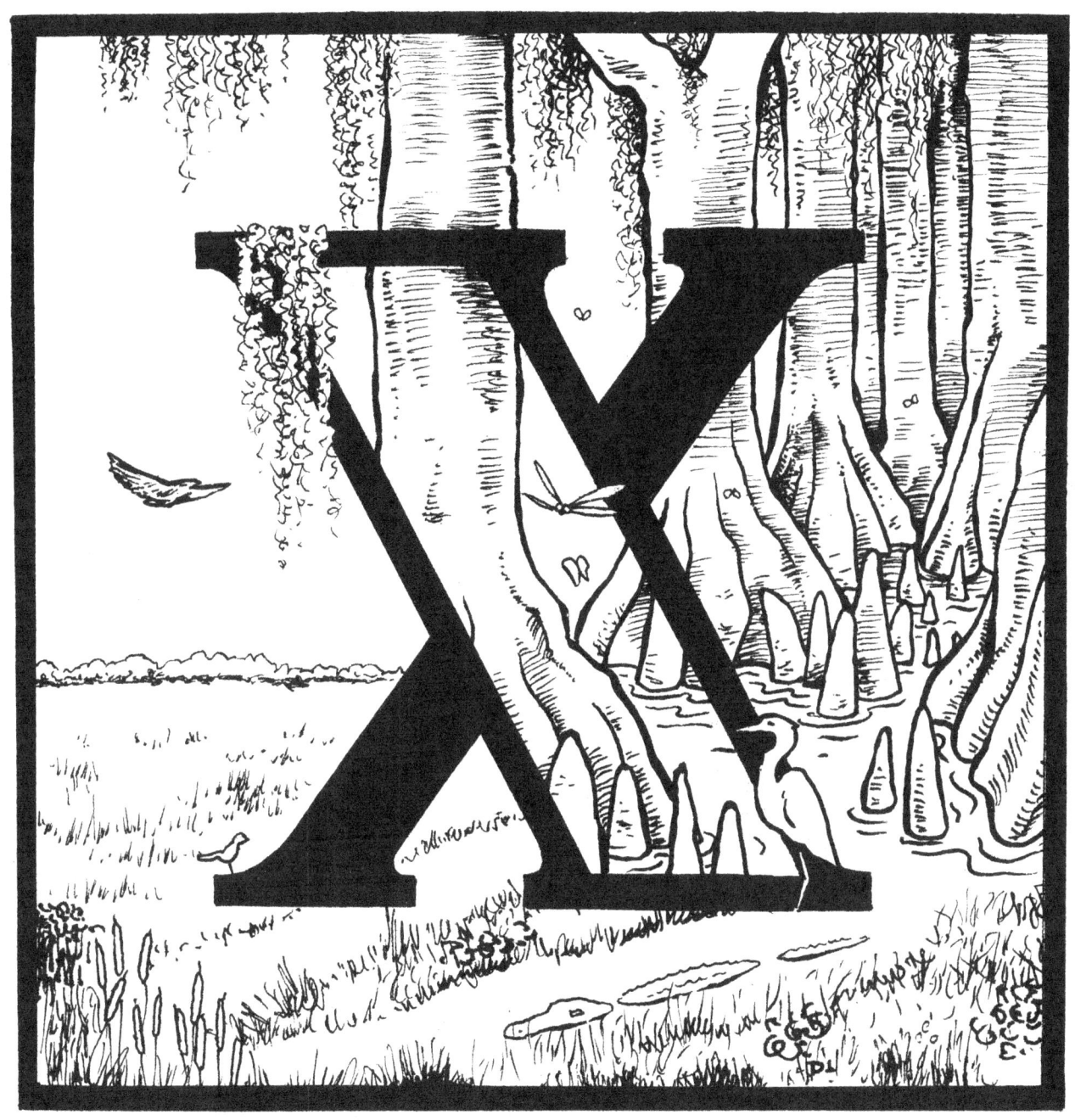

X is for
Xerophytes, the savannah and marsh
which live in watery places
other plants would find harsh.

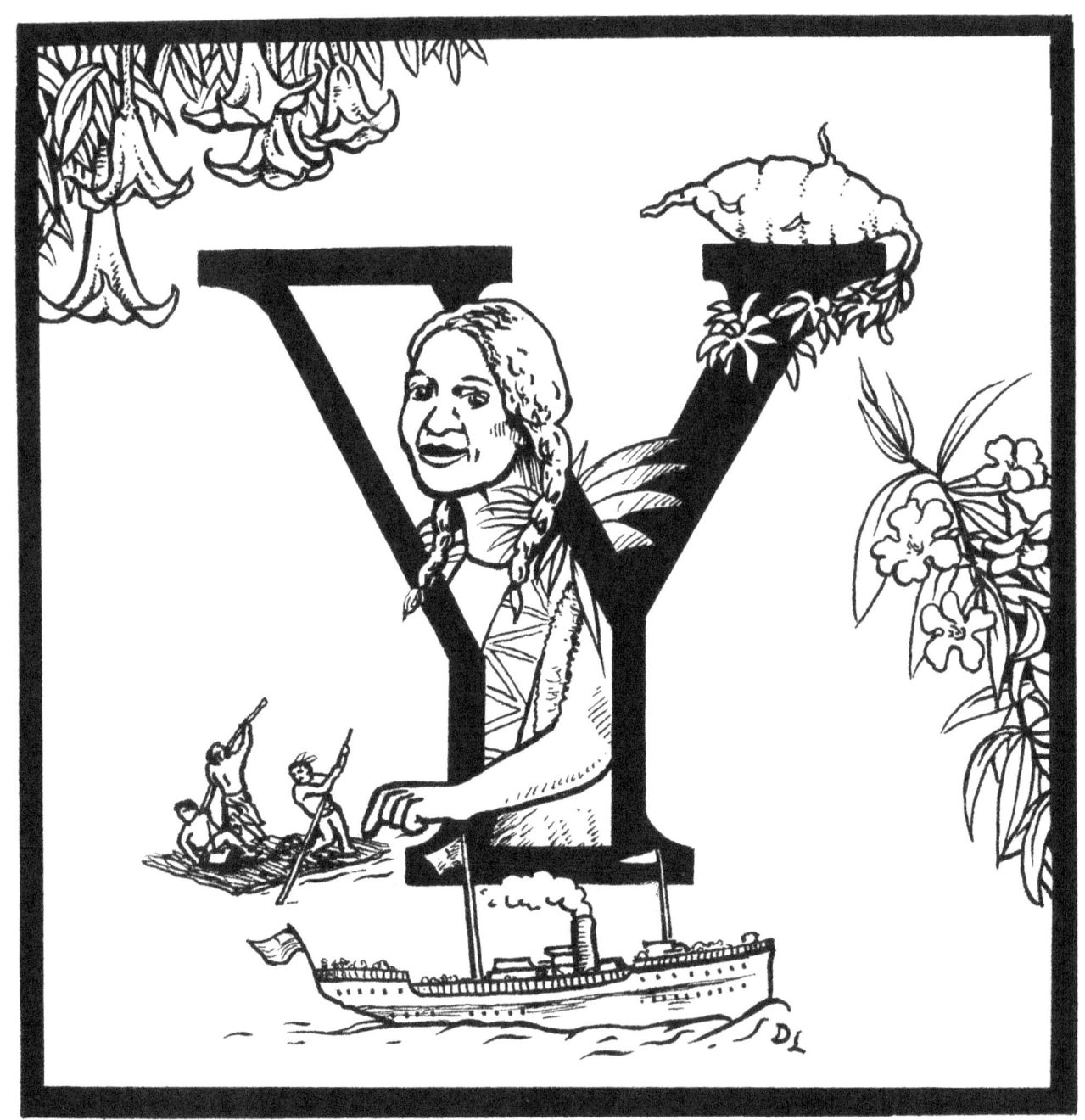

Y is for
Yamacraw, the native tribe of this land.
There are old and new yachts,
yellow flowers and yams.

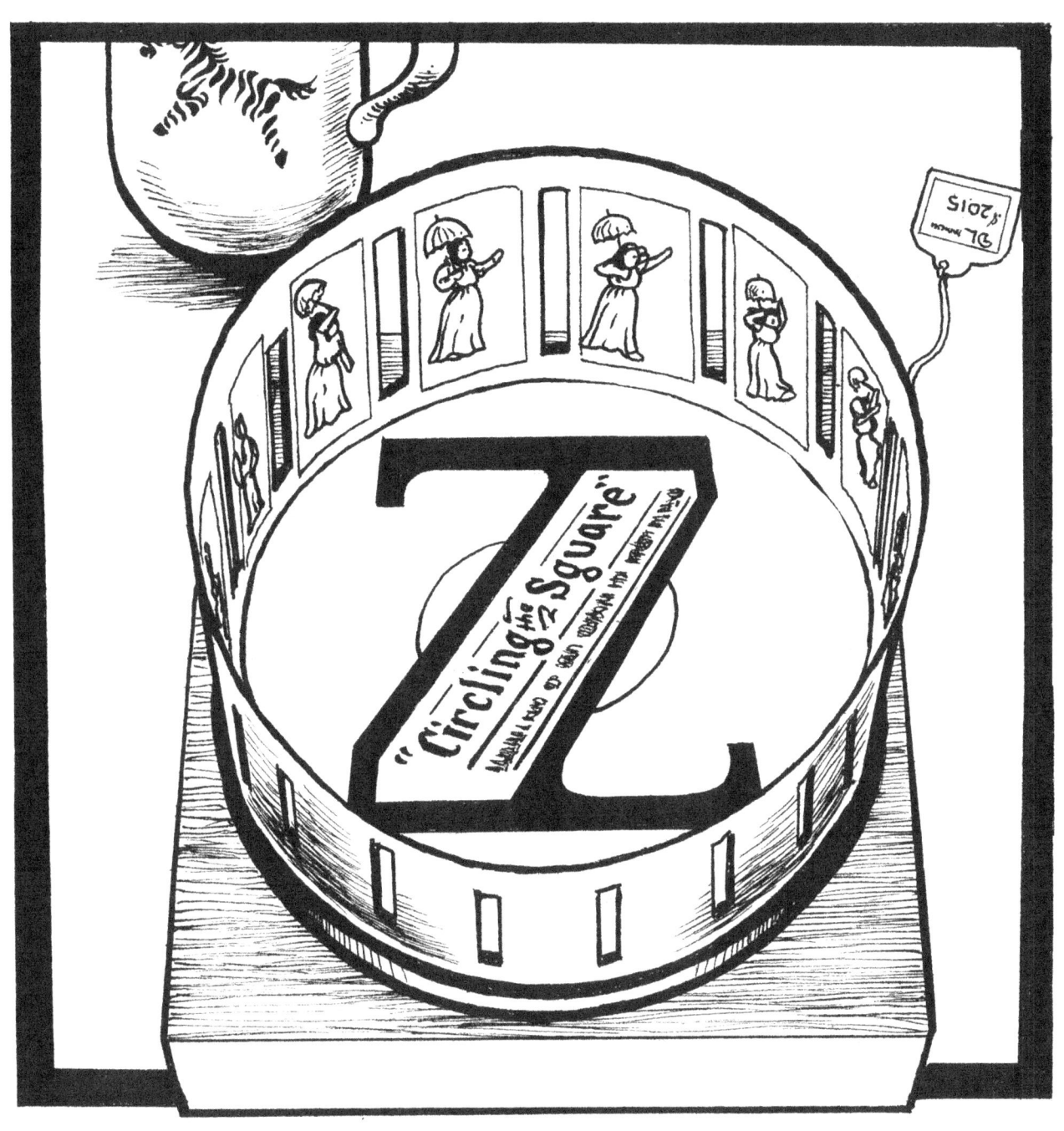

Z is for
Zoetrope, a moving picture device,
that we found in the antique shop.
I told you, Savannah's nice.

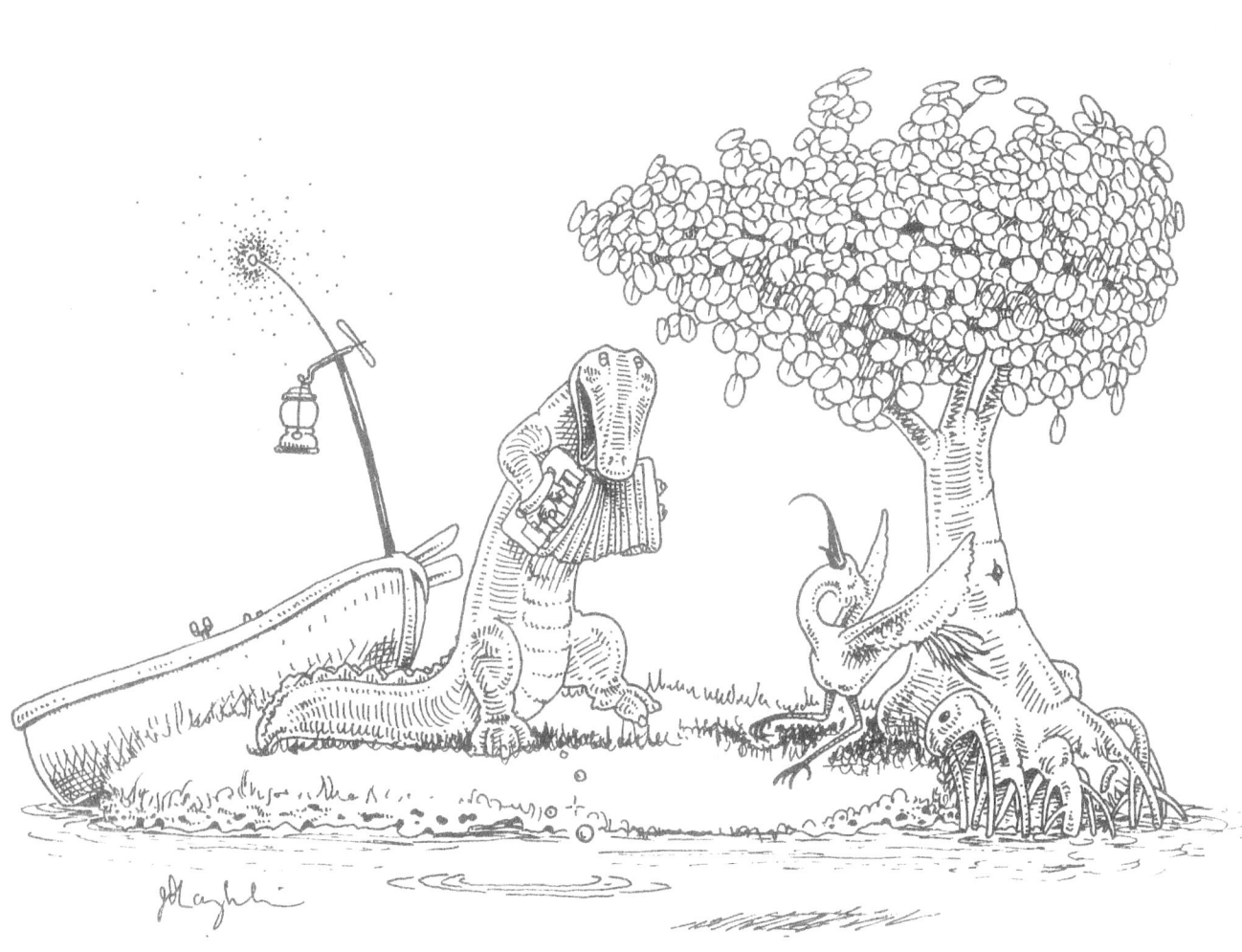

www.ingramcontent.com/pod-product-compliance
Lightning Source LLC
Chambersburg PA
CBHW082304200526
45168CB00017B/3072